Friends Forever

A Tale About Lion and Mouse

Written by Polly Peterson

Illustrated by Sharron O'Neil

One morning, Mouse was on her way
home. She heard a loud, deep sound.

GROWL, SNORE! GROWL, SNORE!

3

What sort of animal would snore like that?
Mouse wanted to know more. She ran to the
sound. The snore got louder and louder.

GROWL, SNORE! GROWL, SNORE!

Mouse saw something in the grass. It looked
like a tail. She went closer to get a good look.

5

What sort of animal would have such a big tail? Mouse wanted to know more. She began to climb up the tail.

The snore was very loud now.

GROWL, SNORE! GROWL, SNORE!

Mouse looked down and saw a huge paw.

7

What sort of animal would have such a
huge paw? Mouse wanted to know more.

Just then, Mouse looked up and saw . . .

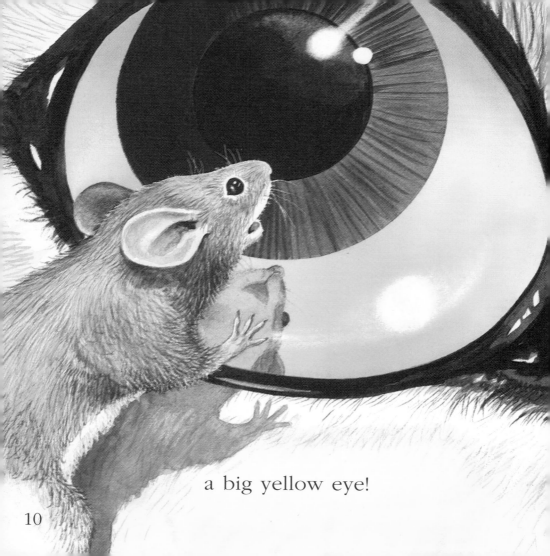

a big yellow eye!

10

She heard a loud **_ROAR!_** Then she knew
just what sort of animal it was.

It was a lion! Mouse jumped down. But
Lion held onto Mouse with his huge paws.

12

"Please let me go," said Mouse.

"Why should I let you go?" said Lion.

"Now that I have you, I am going to eat you."

13

14

"Oh, Lion, what good is it to eat a tiny mouse? You will still need to eat much more. But if you let me go, I will be your friend forever. Someday you may need my help."

"You may go, little Mouse," said Lion.
"But run away before I change my mind."
     Mouse did run away. This time she did
not want to know more.

"Why would a lion need a mouse for help?" said Lion, with a laugh. "Such a thing could never happen!"

Or could it?

Before too long, some hunters came. They
set a trap. It was a big, strong net.

19

That night, Lion stepped into the net. He could not get out. He tugged and tore at the net.

But the more he tugged and tore, the
more the net held him. Lion roared for help.

21

Mouse heard Lion's roar and ran to help.
She knew just what to do.

"Soon you will be free," said Mouse.

Mouse began to chew on the net. She chewed and chewed for a long time. Just before morning, the net tore open. Lion was free!

23

Lion roared once more. This time it was a
happy roar.

"You were right," he said to Mouse. "I did
need your help. You are my friend. We will be
friends forever."